Discover
RUBBER
STAMPING

Discover
RUBBER
STAMPING

LEARN THE

TECHNIQUES AND EFFECTS OF THE SIMPLE ART

OF RUBBER STAMPING

TERRI EARL-McEWEN

and

JENNIE HULME

CHARTWELL
BOOKS, INC.

A QUINTET BOOK

Published by Chartwell Books
A Division of Book Sales, Inc.
114 Northfield Avenue.
Edison, New Jersey 00837

This edition produced for sale in the U.S.A., its
territories and dependencies only.

ISBN 0-7858-0358-0

This book was designed and produced by
Quintet Publishing Limited
6 Blundell Street
London N7 9BH

CREATIVE DIRECTOR: *Richard Dewing*
DESIGNER: *Simon Balley*
PROJECT EDITOR: *Diana Steedman*
EDITOR: *Emma Tolkein*
PHOTOGRAPHER: *Paul Forrester*

Typeset in Great Britain by
Central Southern Typesetters, Eastbourne
Manufactured in Hong Kong by
Regent Publishing Services Ltd.
Printed in China by Leefung-Asco Printers Ltd.

14.99

Contents

INTRODUCTION

The history of rubber stamping dates back to the mid 1860s. Although seals have been used on official documents since ancient times and rubber has been used since the 17th century, historians cannot agree on exactly who made the first stamp. Traditionally stamps were created for business use, however in the mid 1970s the art community in the United States began experimenting with picture stamps.

Today, art stamping is found world wide. The craft itself has grown as more uses are found for the rubber stamp. Though most people associate stamping with paper, they can also be used on other materials such as wood, fabric and clays. Uses also include T-shirt printing, jewelry making and even the decoration of some food items. The applications for rubber stamping are only limited by the user's own imagination.

This book has been compiled as an introduction to the art of rubber stamping. The step by step projects are easy to follow for the novice, as well as for the experienced stamper and should provide some inspiration for you to develop your own ideas and style.

GETTING
STARTED

To start stamping a few basic items are required. A good starter kit would include the following:

A STAMP When selecting that first stamp, look for a design that can be used for a number of different projects. Many different designs are available these days from both art and craft shops. Indeed stamps representing characters from children's books and films can also be found in newsagents and toy shops. The designs available range from the simplest individual letters to complicated and intricate patterns. The projects described here list specific stamps for each task. If you have any trouble getting hold of any of them then a list of manufacturers and stockists is given at the end of the book for the stamps used in each project. Obviously as you become more proficient and experienced you will want to experiment with various other patterns and move on from the suggestions given here.

FELT-TIP PENS Select pens that have a broad tip and are water based. These pens can be used for coloring directly onto the stamp as well as for coloring in a printed design.

COLORED PENCILS These can also be used to color in a printed design.

WATERCOLORS A set of watercolor paints can also be used for coloring a printed design and the paints can be applied directly onto the rubber for printing.

GLITTER Glitters are used as an accessory, and give a finished design a touch of sparkle. Glitters come in a variety of colors and can be found both loose or suspended in glue.

GLUE A water based glue pen is an essential item to have in any craft box.

INK PADS Inks can be found in a variety of colors and types. Regular, or endorsing, inks are a fast drying ink, similar to the inks used in the business place. Pigment inks are a

thick creamy ink that are slow drying. They are ideal for use with most projects including embossing onto fabrics. Embossing inks are a lightly tinted or colorless ink. They are slow drying which is essential for good embossing results.

EMBOSSING POWDERS *Embossing powders are available in metallic, transparent and colored finishes. The powder is a heat sensitive compound that solidifies when exposed to extreme temperatures resulting in a raised image.*

TOOLS

You may already have the basic tools but to complete the projects in this book it will be necessary to have the following:

SCISSORS *A pair of sharp scissors are an essential tool for most crafts. There are also a wide range of scissors which* cut out decorative patterns and you may find these useful. Deckle edged scissors cut a random pattern and are an easy way to create a feathered edging.

CRAFT KNIFE *The craft knife is also an essential tool for most crafts.*

RULER *A ruler is usually needed for measuring out paper sizes. A metal edge is ideal for use with the craft knife for cutting straight lines.*

CUTTING BOARD *The cutting board is designed to protect your work surfaces. A board with square markings will make it easier to cut straight sides.*

HEAT TOOL *A source of heat will be required to emboss. A paint stripper was used for the projects in this book, however, the same results can be achieved from an iron, a hot plate or even a spotlight.*

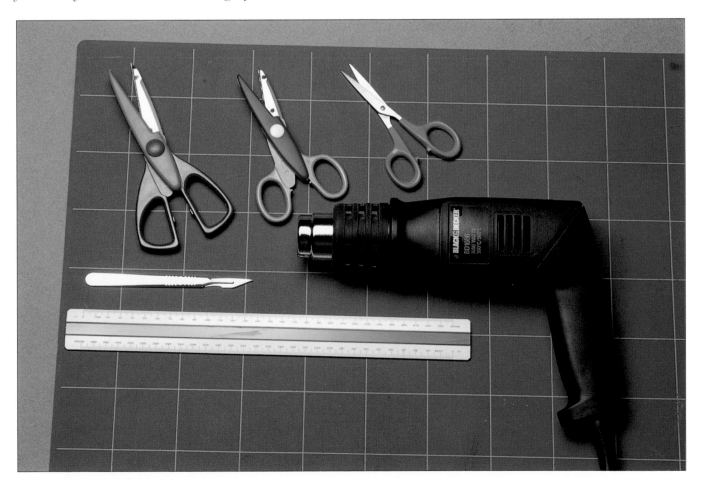

CARE OF STAMPS AND INKS

STAMPS *Although rubber is durable care is needed when using and cleaning the stamps. Oil based products should be avoided as these will damage the rubber. Stamps should be cleaned after use as not only does this prolong the life of the stamp but it also helps to keep your storage box clean. Cleaning stamps is easy. Take a piece of wet kitchen towel and place it on a tray, place a dry piece of kitchen towel next to it. To clean off the ink, stamp a couple of times onto the wet paper, then on the dry paper. Commercial stamp cleaners are also available. They are usually found in a bottle with a sponge applicator. Do not wash the inks off under running water or use any harsh chemicals. An old, soft toothbrush may be used to clean dirt and ink from the crevices.*

STORING STAMPS *Sunlight is not kind to rubber. To prolong a stamp's life, it is recommended that they are stored away from direct sunlight. A tool box is ideal for storage, though there are special boxes available.*

If new to this craft, begin by selecting a simple stamp that is representative of you, or a design that can be used for a number of different things. More specific stamps can be added once the techniques have been mastered. When stamping, select a work surface that is smooth and firm as printing on a textured or soft surface will affect the results.

BASIC
STAMPING

P*rinting stamps can be done either with an ink pad or by using water based felt-tip pens directly onto the stamp.*

USING INK PADS

❶ Using an ink pad, ink the stamp, checking that it is fully covered before printing. With larger stamps it may be easier to apply the pad to the stamp, as this helps avoid over-inking, especially when using pigment inks.

❷ Print the stamp by placing it straight down onto a card. Apply the necessary pressure. (Less pressure is required for more delicate stamps and more pressure for the bolder ones.) Avoid rocking and rolling the stamp as this may blur the image. With practice you will be able to judge how much pressure is needed.

❸ Remove the stamp by lifting it straight off the paper.

USING FELT-TIP PENS

For this method ensure your pens are water based. Do not use oil based pens as they may damage the rubber of the stamp.

❶ Using a felt-tip pen color directly onto the rubber stamp. More than one color may be used at any one time, however it will be necessary to work quickly as the inks are fast drying.

❷ Prior to printing the stamp, huff on the image to moisten any dried inks, then print in the same manner as the ink pad method.

COLORING THE IMAGES

Once a stamp has been printed additional color may be applied to finish the design. Felt-tip pens, water colors or colored pencils may be used.

GLITTERING

Glitter adds an extra sparkle to any design. Glitter glue (glitter suspended in glue) or loose glitter can be used. Glitter glue is applied directly onto the design but practice first as some glitter glues can blot. To apply the loose glitter put small amounts of glue on the design and shake the glitter over the

image. It is best to work over a plastic container as this minimizes glitter spilling onto the work surface. Or spread a large sheet of paper under your work so that the surplus glitter can be poured back into the container. With either method, allow enough time for the glue to dry before handling.

ADVICE ABOUT PAPER

The paper chosen to stamp on can make a difference in the final results. It is advisable to avoid high gloss papers, textured papers or papers that are very absorbent (recycled paper). High gloss or coated papers smudge very easily when stamped whereas textured papers make it difficult to get an even print. Absorbent papers, on the other hand, may bleed giving a blurred image. For the best results start with a smooth, plain finished card or paper until consistent results are achieved … then experiment! A description of some of the different papers you may want to use can be found on page 94.

BASIC

TECHNIQUES

MASKING

Masking is a technique used to print overlapping images. To make a mask, self adhesive, reusable sticky notepads are very useful.

1 Stamp the design onto the paper.

2 To make a mask stamp the same design onto a sticky note, ensuring the image is positioned close to the sticky portion of the pad as the adhesive will need to be used. Carefully cut it out.

3 Place the mask directly over the first design.

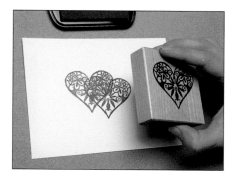

4 Stamp the design again, overlapping the first. (This could be done in a contrasting color.)

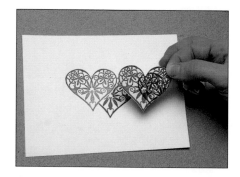

5 Remove the mask.

R EPETITION

Repetition is a technique often used to create wrapping papers. This technique could also be used to add a border to writing paper, or to decorate cards.

❶ Ink the stamp and print it out.

❷ Re-ink the stamp and print again at regular intervals to make a continuous pattern.

STREAKING

Streaking is a technique that gives the impression of movement.

❶ Determine which direction the design should streak. Ink the stamp and print it on to the card. Without lifting it drag the stamp across the card in the desired direction and, in one movement, lift the stamp at the end. Do not stop the stamp before lifting as this may leave a shadow image.

FADING OUT

Like streaking this technique shows movement.

❶ Ink a stamp and print it onto the card. Without re-inking print the design again, this time a fraction to the side of the original print. Continue printing, without re-inking, each time moving the image just a fraction from the last print so that the image appears to be fading away.

COMBINING DESIGNS

*Combining designs is a technique where two or more stamps
are used to create a picture.*

1 Select two stamps that work well together
such as two flowers or this bear and balloon.
Ink and stamp out the first image.

2 Decide where the second image should be
placed, ink the stamp and then print. (For
some combinations the masking technique
may be useful.) Experiment with using the
same, similar or different colors for each
stamp.

STAMPS AND STENCILS

Stamps can be used to create interesting effects when combined with stencils.

❶ Cut a stencil such as this heart shape, and place it on the card. Using a simple patterned stamp fill in the area of the stencil by repeatedly printing the design.

❷ Remove the stencil and check the image. If it needs more filling replace and continue stamping until the desired effect is achieved.

The same process can be used in reverse. Simply use the stencil cut-out and stamp around it.

3 D

*This is a simple technique that can be used to give a design
that three-dimensional look.*

1 Print the design on a card.

2 On another piece of card print the design again, then carefully cut out the portion of the design that will be raised.

3 Attach a sticky fixer to the back of the cut-out. Position this over the original image and stick in place so that it will be slightly raised.

POP-UP CARDS

Here are two techniques that will make any card pop!

TECHNIQUE ONE

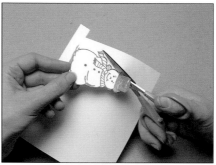

1 Print the design on a piece of card and carefully cut it out.

2 Using a narrow strip of card, fold it into a square. Cut off the excess, and fasten together.

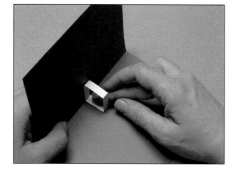

3 Position the pop-up mechanism in the fold of a card and secure to both sides of the card.

4 Fasten the cut out design to the front of the mechanism. As the card is opened so your picture will open with it.

TECHNIQUE TWO

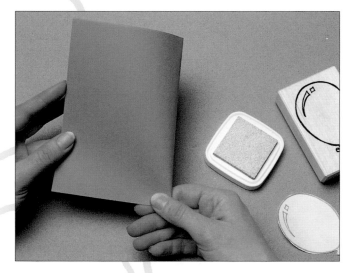

1 Find the center of the card, but do not crease at this stage. The best way to find the center is to bend the card in half and just pinch together the top and bottom of the fold.

2 Print the design, ensuring a portion of the image overlaps the center of the card.

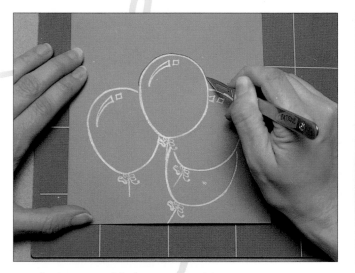

3 To finish, use a craft knife to cut around the portion of the design that is above the center line of the card.

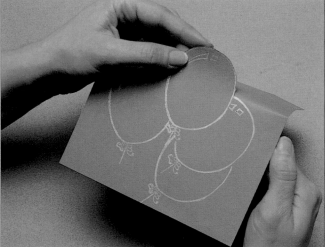

4 Fold the card, ensuring the cut out portion remains straight.

REVERSE IMAGE

This technique requires a mirror image stamp, that is a stamp that is simply a smooth piece of rubber. Select a stamp that faces either right or left so that the image can be clearly and easily reversed.

❶ Print a design onto the card.

❷ Re-ink the stamp and print it onto the mirror image stamp.

❸ Using the mirror image stamp, position and print out a reverse image so that, as in this illustration for instance, the two fish appear to be swimming towards each other.

SPONGING

*Sponging is a technique that can be done directly onto the
stamp before you use it to print, or it can be used to color in a
finished design.*

SPONGING THE COLOR

❶ Print out the design, and allow the ink to dry.

❷ Ink up a piece of cosmetic sponge by
dabbing it onto an ink pad. It is advisable to
use a color that is different from the first and
then dab the sponge onto the design until you
are satisfied with the result.

SPONGING ONTO A STAMP

1 Ink up a cosmetic sponge as before and apply the color directly onto the stamp. More than one color may be used either next to each other or blended with one another.

2 Once the stamp is fully inked then you can print it out.

EMBOSSING

Embossing is a very simple technique with extraordinary results though it can be disappointing if it is not done correctly. A heat source is needed for this technique. Heat the powdered image until the powder melts but note that it is the image only that is held near the heat.

1 Ink the stamp and print it out onto the card. Either embossing ink, which is colorless, or pigment inks may be used.

2 While the image is still wet, pour embossing powder over it. It is important to do this while the ink is still wet, otherwise the powder will not stick. Shake off the excess.

3 Heat the powdered image until the powder melts. This should take approximately 15–20 seconds depending on the intensity of the heat. Avoid over-heating as this will make the image appear flat and waxy.

4 As soon as all the powder has melted the process is complete.

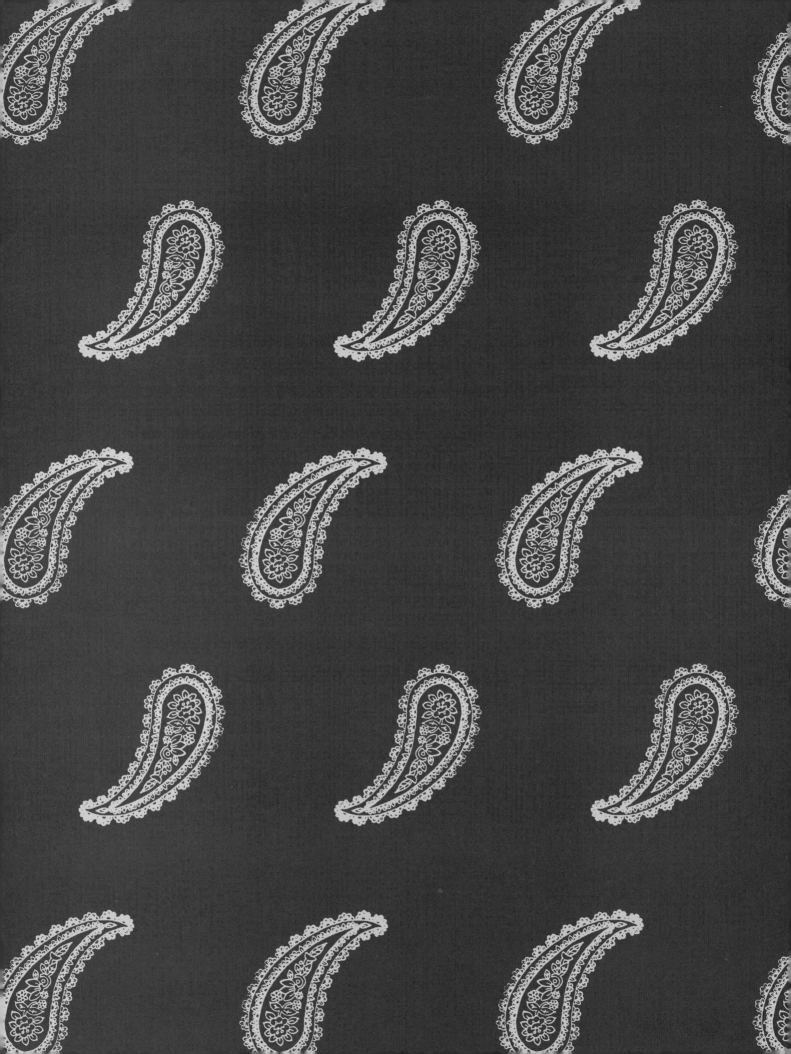

BASIC
PROJECTS

WRAPPING PAPER

To make this striking wrapping paper the following items will be required:

- 1 sheet of turquoise tissue paper
- Silver pigment ink pad

STAMPS *Floral paisley*

❶ Cut the paper to fit the parcel.

❷ Using the repetition technique print out a row of the paisley stamp, curve side up. Skip a space of approximately 1½ in and print out a second row. Repeat this until the end of the paper is reached.

❸ Turning the stamp so the curved side is down, print out a row in the space between the existing rows.

❹ After the ink has dried you can wrap and decorate the parcel.

GIFT TAGS

T o create this simple yet individual gift tag is easy. The following items will be required:

- Packet of ready made gift tags
- Cream paper 1¾ in x 3 in
- Green mulberry paper 1¾ in x 3 in
- Deckle-edged scissors
- Greenery pigment ink pad
- Self-adhesive reusable sticky note pad
- Glue

STAMPS *Maple leaf*

1 Stamp out leaf design onto sticky note pad to make a mask. Carefully cut it out and place to one side.

2 On 1¾ in x 3 in cream paper, print out leaf in the darkest green color. Clean the ink off the stamp.

3 Place mask over the print and, using the medium color green, print to the right of the original, slightly overlapping the first leaf. Clean the stamp.

4 Leaving the mask in place, ink the stamp using the lightest color and print it to the left of the original. Remove the mask.

⑤ Using the deckle-edged scissors cut the mulberry paper to ⅓ in smaller than the packaged gift tag.

⑥ Glue the mulberry paper onto the gift tag.

⑦ Carefully cut out the printed leaves and, centering them on the mulberry paper, glue in place.

CARDS – COMBINING DESIGNS

*T*his underwater scene is easy to make and would make the perfect greeting card for any fish lover. The following items will be needed:

- Paper: green Italian recycled paper 5¾ in x 4 in
  blue Italian recycled paper 5¾ in x 4 in
  cream card sized 10 in x 7 in
  small piece of cream card approximately
  1 in x 2 in
- Embossing ink
- Gold embossing powder
- Silver embossing powder
- Wavy scissors

STAMPS *Eric the fish, Little fish, Seaweed*

- Heat tool
- Glue
- Assortment of felt-tip pens
- Sticky fixers

❶ Glue the blue paper on to the front of the cream card.

❷ Using an embossing ink pad, print both seaweed designs across the bottom of the green paper, alternating them.

❸ Sprinkle with gold embossing powder and heat.

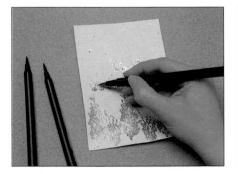

❹ In the space above the seaweed print out the little fish with embossing ink, repeating the design to make a shoal. Emboss the shoal using the silver powder.

❺ Cut the top of the green paper using the wavy scissors and, positioning over the blue paper, glue in place. Add a touch of color to the fish with the felt-tip pens.

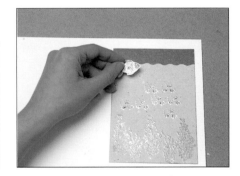

❻ On the small piece of cream paper print and emboss Eric the fish in gold. Color in the embossed design with bright, felt-tip pens, then carefully cut out the design. Apply a sticky fixer to the back and position onto the top of the green paper.

3D CARD

T his simple yet elegant card would be a delight for your
Mom on Mother's Day. To make this card you will
require the following:

- Paper: cream card 3¾ in x 5½ in
        orange card 8¼ in x 5¾ in
        burgundy card 3¾ in x 5½ in
- Embossing ink pad
- Gold embossing powder
- Craft knife
- Felt-tip pens: pink, cranberry, purple, yellow and green
- Sticky fixers
- Glue

STAMPS *Floral wreath*

- Heat tool

① Position the burgundy card on the orange card as illustrated and glue in place.

② Print out two Floral wreaths on cream card and emboss in gold.

③ Color one wreath completely using the felt-tip pens. Color only the purple flowers on the second wreath.

④ Using a craft knife, carefully cut out the colored wreath. Place to one side. On the second wreath cut out only the purple colored flowers.

⑤ Position and glue the full wreath onto the burgundy card.

⑥ Using sticky fixers position the individual flowers over their matching flowers on the first wreath and fix in place. Fold the card in half and it is now ready for your message.

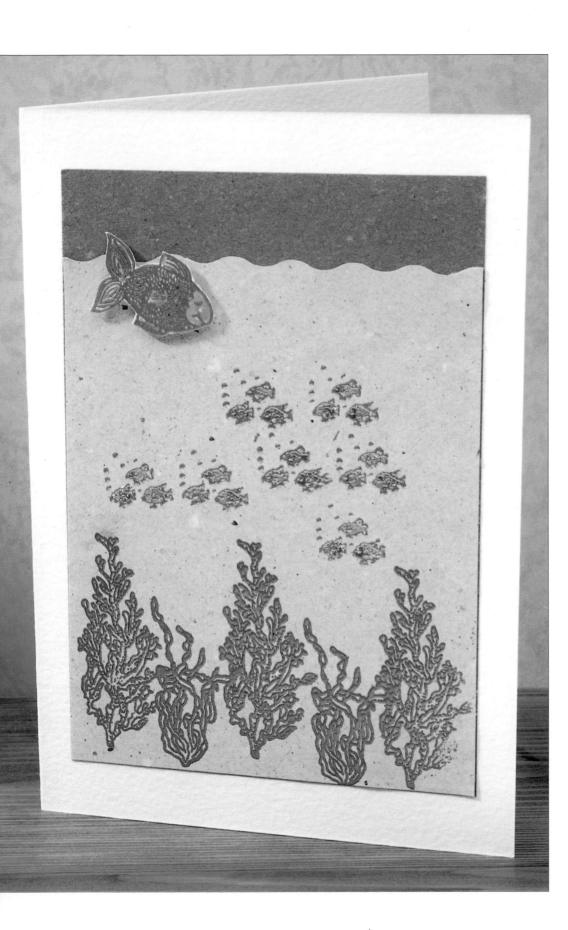

POP-UP CARD

B*oth pop-up techniques have been used to create this colorful card. To make this card you will need:*

- Bright blue card 5¾ in x 8¼ in
- Bright yellow card 5¾ in x 4 in
- Bright pink card 5¾ in x 4 in
- Bright turquoise card 5¾ in x 4 in
- Cream card 5¾ in x 4 in
- Bright embroidery cottons
- Embossing ink pad
- Silver embossing powder
- Scissors
- Craft knife
- Sticky fixers
- Felt-tip pens: light brown and hot pink
- **STAMPS** *Large balloon, T-shirt bear*
- Heat tool

  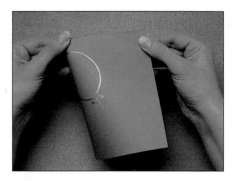

❶ On the cream card print and emboss the teddy bear. At the same time print and emboss the balloon onto the pink, turquoise and yellow cards. Carefully cut out each of the embossed images and place to one side.

❷ On the bright blue card, position the balloon stamp as shown, print and emboss.

❸ Find the center fold of the card by bending the card and pinching the top and bottom of the fold. Do not crease the card yet. Using a craft knife, carefully cut out around the left side of the balloon. (Using the fold line as a starting and finishing point.) Leaving the cut out portion of the balloon straight, crease the card.

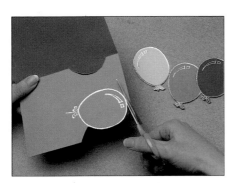 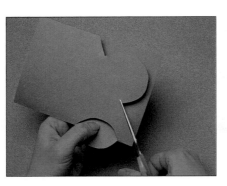 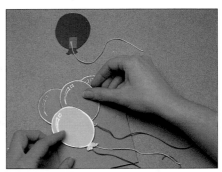

4 On the inside of the card emboss another balloon in the upper right hand corner of the card. Carefully cutting around the balloon, cut out the upper corner of the card.

5 Using the same diagonal line, carefully cut away the front upper corner of the card, being careful to avoid the first balloon.

6 Take the other colored balloons embossed earlier, and attach a length of embroidery cotton and a sticky fixer to the back of each of them. On the front of the card position the turquoise and yellow balloons as shown and fix in place.

 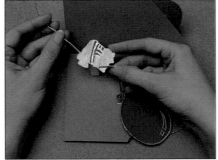

7 Position the pink balloon on the inside of the card and fix in place. Using a strip of cream card, make a pop-up mechanism, and fix to the card as shown.

8 Position and attach the teddy bear to the mechanism, and finally pull the cottons through the bear's paws.

STATIONERY

*C*hildren can have hours of fun creating their own
personalized stationery. To create this stationery the
following is needed:

- Set of neon writing paper and matching envelopes
- Pigment ink pads: cyan blue, pink, navy, purple

STAMPS *Lion, Elephant, Monkey, Mirror image stamp*

1 Find the center of the paper and mark it lightly. Ink the lion stamp, using cyan blue on the head and navy on the body. On the bottom of the paper, position the stamp over the center and print.

2 Using navy ink print the elephant on the right hand side of the lion.

3 Ink the elephant stamp again and print onto the mirror image stamp, then position the mirror image stamp on the left side of the lion and print so that both elephants are looking at the lion.

4 To print the envelopes, print a purple elephant in the lower right corner. Then on the mirror image stamp first, print a purple elephant, then print a pink monkey on his back. Position and print in the lower left corner of the envelope. To finish the stationery collection print a lion on the flap of the envelope.

PARTY INVITATION

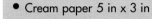

*T*his bright and festive invitation will suit the celebration of almost any occasion and the following two projects will enable you to continue the theme of the party. To create this invitation the following items will be required:

- Cream paper 5 in x 3 in
- Green paper 5¾ in x 8¼ in
- Red paper 5½ in x 3½ in

STAMPS *Star burst, Crown*

- Crystal embossing powder
- Symphonic pigment ink pad
- Deckle-edged scissors
- Glue
- Heat tool

❶ Ink the star burst stamp using the blue and green portion of the pad. With a piece of scrap paper underneath, print around the edge of the cream paper, overlapping it.

❷ Using the yellow and red section of the pad ink up the crown stamp and print in the center of the cream card. Emboss the crown with the crystal embossing powder.

❸ Trim the edge of the cream card with the deckle-edged scissors.

❹ Position and glue the red paper onto the green card. Finish by positioning the cream card onto the red paper and glue in place. The card is now ready for you to write in it.

PAPER BAGS

*T*o make these party bags the following will be required:

- Colored paper bag
- Cream card 5¾ in x 4 in
- Silver pigment ink pad
- Symphonic pigment ink pad
- Crystal embossing powder

STAMPS *Frame, Crown*

- Cosmetic sponge
- Sticky fixers
- Scissors
- Heat tool

❶ Using the yellow and red section of the symphonic pad, ink the crown and print it onto the cream paper.

❷ Emboss the crown with the crystal embossing powder, then carefully cut it out and set it aside.

❸ Ink the frame stamp with the silver ink and print onto the top portion of the bag.

❹ Ink the cosmetic sponge with the silver ink and sponge a cloud below the frame on the bag.

❺ Attach a sticky fixer to the back of the crown, position it on the cloud and secure it. Finish by adding the recipient's name inside the frame.

PARTY HATS

*C*reate the crowning glory for that special birthday person. To create this crown the following will be required:

- Yellow card 2 ft x 3 ft
- Cream card 5¾ in x 4 in
- Symphonic pigment ink pad
- Black pigment ink pad
- Shredded colored paper

STAMPS *Clown, Big balloon*

- Dark blue yarn 4 in
- Sticky fixers
- Cosmetic sponge
- Scissors
- Craft knife
- Pencil
- Tape

1 Using the full length of the yellow card, draw out the shape of the crown and carefully cut it out.

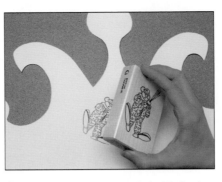

2 Ink up the clown stamp with the black ink and print on to the center of the crown. Set aside to allow the ink time to dry.

3 Using the black ink print out two balloons onto the cream card.

4 Ink the cosmetic sponge with blue and green ink, and sponge the color onto one of the balloons. Color the second balloon in the same manner, using the reds and oranges. Carefully cut out both balloons.

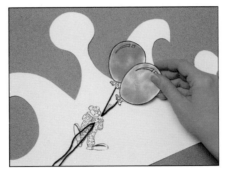

5 Cut the length of yarn in half and tape each half to a balloon. Using the craft knife, carefully cut a slit at the top of the clown's hands, as well as one on the bottom. Attach a sticky fixer to the back of each balloon, position them on the crown and fix in place. Thread the yarn through the slits, and trim.

6 Take a small bunch of shredded paper and tape to the back of each of the peaks on the crown. Finish by sizing the hat to fit.

BOOKMARK

T his cheery bookmark would make a lovely place saver
for any book worm. To make this the following will
be required:

- Dark yellow card 6 in x 2 in
- Cream card 5½ in x 1½ in

STAMPS *Sun flower*

- Felt-tip pens: yellow, orange and green
- Hole punch
- Deckle-edged scissors
- Blue embroidery cotton
- Glue
- Scissors

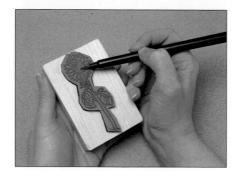

❶ Ink the stamp using the felt-tip pens. Color
the flower with the orange, and the leaves and
stem with the green. Huff on the stamp to
moisten the inks before printing on to the
cream card.

2 Color in the printed sun flower, with the felt-tips.

3 Trim the edge of the yellow card with the deckle-edged scissors, then position the cream card onto the yellow and glue in place.

4 To finish, punch a hole in the top of the card and thread the embroidery cotton through.

ADVANCED
TECHNIQUES

STAINED GLASS WORK OR DOUBLE EMBOSSING

Stained glass work is a technique where both the image and the colored-in areas are embossed. The finished result looks like a stained glass window.

1 Print the design with embossing ink and emboss with black embossing powder. Alternatively, clear embossing powder may be used over black pigment ink.

2 Color the design with felt-tip pens.

3 Paint a thin coat of embossing ink or a clear glue over the colored areas, and repowder the image with clear embossing powder.

4 Heat the image until the powder melts to complete the process.

WATERCOLORING

Watercolors can be used directly on the stamp, or they can be used to colour an embossed image.

WATERCOLORING ONTO STAMPS

❶ Paint directly onto the stamp with watercolors. It is advisable to keep the paints as thick and as wet as possible.

❷ Once the painting is finished, give a quick dab with a damp brush, to any dried areas, and huff onto the stamp to make sure it is still damp.

❸ Print out the design either on plain paper or onto prepared watercolor paper.

WATERCOLORING
AN EMBOSSED IMAGE

❶ Emboss a design on a card or prepared watercolor paper.

❷ Using watercolors paint the image. For a subtler finish use a thinner consistency of paint.

Rubber stamping is a versatile craft. With a little imagination, and not restricting it to the bounds of paper or card but using many different materials, there is no end to what can be stamped. The following techniques are all done on mediums other than paper.

FABRIC PAINTING

Customized fabric can be printed by using fabric inks and paints with the stamps. Pigment inks may also be used for embossing on fabric.

To print with fabric inks, select a suitable fabric as recommended by the manufacturer, and plan out the design.

1 Secure the prepared fabric in a frame. (If a frame is not available, cotton fabrics may be smoothed over a piece of sandpaper to prevent slipping.)

2 Ink up the stamp and print onto the fabric. Follow the instructions for the steadfastness of the ink.

EMBOSSING ONTO FABRIC

Transparent embossing powders can be used over pigment inks to seal them onto the fabric. Remember the embossing powder is a plastic and so the fabric will require special handling after you have finished your design.

1 Secure the fabric in a frame as in the previous technique. Please note that for this technique a frame should be used to hold the fabric steady as you will need to turn it over. Ink the stamp with a pigment ink and print onto the fabric.

2 Pour some embossing powder over the image.

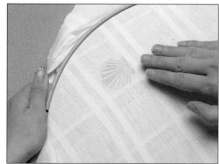

3 Remove the excess by tapping the back of the fabric.

4 Heat the embossing powder. Please note that the powder usually melts faster on fabric than on paper so watch overheating.

INTERIOR DECORATION PRINTING ON WOOD

Stamps may be used to decorate wooden items such as cutting boards and salt boxes or pieces of furniture.

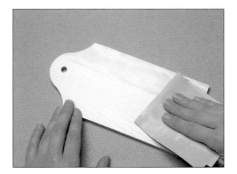

1 Prepare the wood surface by cleaning and sanding.

2 Ink the stamp as desired and print onto the prepared surface.

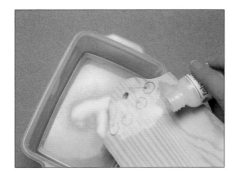

If desired the design may also be embossed. To emboss, pour the powder over the image while it is still wet, and heat to melt. Avoid overheating.

USING STAMPS AS STENCILS

Rubber stamps may also be used to decorate walls instead of using stencils. A wall with a smooth finish is ideal, whereas printing onto a textured wall will give results similar to printing onto textured papers which can be interesting though unexpected. Stenciling paints or acrylic paints may be used.

❶ Ink the stamp by sponging or rolling the paint onto the stamp.

❷ Print onto the wall. If using a large stamp place the stamp onto the wall and hit the center of the stamp with a fist. Then lift the stamp away from the wall. This is an easy method that achieves an even print. Avoid rocking and rolling the stamp on the wall as this will distort the image.

STAMPING ONTO FOOD

....

Food can take on a new and decorative look with edible food
colorings.

❶ Using a basic sugar cookie recipe, cut out
the cookies in the desired shape.

❷ Ink the stamp using food coloring pens and
press into the dough.

❸ The stamp will need to be cleaned between
stampings as a residue from the dough will
lessen the color of the next print.

❹ Cook the cookies as instructed in the
recipe. *Bon appetit!*

JEWELRY MAKING

Unusual and unique jewelry can be made using rubber stamps.

STAMPING ONTO CLAY

Rubber stamps can be used with polymer clays to create a range of jewelry. There are two methods of printing into the clay and, dependant on the color of the clay used, one may be more effective than the other.

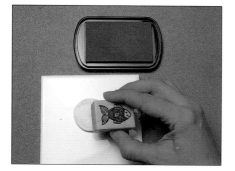

❶ For either method roll out a piece of clay to the required size on a smooth tile.

❷ Ink the stamp and press it into the clay.

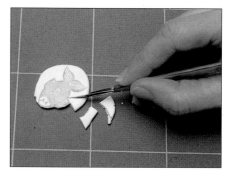

❸ Using a craft knife, carefully cut out the image, and follow the manufacturer's instructions for baking.

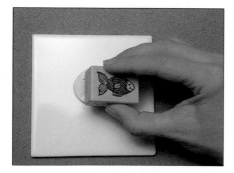

For the second method,

❷ Press an uninked stamp into the clay.

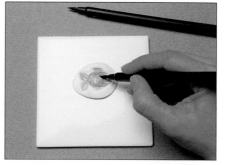

❸ Use felt-tip pens to color the image. Finish as described in step three of the first method.

SHRINK PLASTIC JEWELRY

To perform this technique a special plastic material is required.
The result can be a favorite design in miniature.

❶ Score the shrink plastic sheet lightly with sandpaper.

❷ Stamp the design using either fabric ink or a permanent ink.

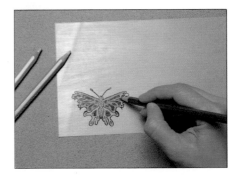

❸ Color in the design using pencils or crayons.

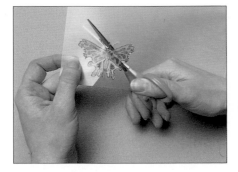

❹ Carefully cut out the design. If required, a hole will need to be punched in the plastic at this stage.

❺ Place the jewelry onto a baking tray and heat in a 275°F oven for 3-5 minutes, until the plastic has shrunk.

❻ It may be necessary to flatten the design upon removal from the oven if it has curled up.

ADVANCED
PROJECTS

CHRISTMAS CARDS

*C*elebrate the festive season with this bright card. The
following items will be needed:

- Cream card 4 in x 5½ in
- Turquoise card 10¼ in x 6¼ in
- Embossing ink
- Embossing pad
- Clear embossing powder
- Black embossing powder
- Felt-tip pens: red, bright green and dark green

STAMPS *Poinsettia wreath*

- Paint brush
- Glue
- Heat tool

❶ Ink the stamp with the embossing ink and print onto the cream card.

❷ Pour the black embossing powder over the wet image, tap off the excess, and heat.

❸ Color in the embossed design, using the felt-tip pens.

❹ Using the embossing ink, paint a thin coat of ink over the colored areas.

❺ Powder the image with the clear embossing powder and heat.

❻ To finish, position the cream card on the turquoise card and glue in place.

WATERCOLOR PICTURE

To create this country scene the following will be required:

- Box frame: A6 size box with 1½ in wide frame
- Watercolor paints
- Block of watercolor paper: 5¾ in x 4 in

SCENIC STAMPS *Hill, Trees, Fields, Row of houses, Church, Pub, Row of shrubs, Clump of trees*

- Scissors
- Craft knife
- Rule

❶ Using watercolors paint directly onto the stamps and print the hill and the fields onto the paper. Using the diluted colors paint the sky and fill in the images.

❷ Using the tree and house row stamps, print with watercolors onto a second piece of paper. On a third piece of paper print out another scene using the shrub stamp, the tree clump, the church, and the church stamp.

❸ Use diluted watercolors to paint the backgrounds on each print, and to fill in the images.

4 Carefully trim the hill scene so it fits snugly into the back of the box. Glue in place. Carefully cut around the tops of the trees on the second scene, and around the top of the shrubs on the third. Ensure enough excess card is left at the bottom of each for a tab.

5 Using a craft knife score along the bottom of the back of the scenes ½ in from the bottom edge.

6 To assemble, bend along the score marks, attach a piece of double-sided sticky tape to the bottom of the tabs, position in the frame and secure each layer in place. To finish the picture position the frame on the box and secure in place.

WEDDING INVITATION

To make this elegant wedding invitation the following will be required:

- Tracing paper 3½ in x 5 in
- White card 4 in x 11 in
- Yellow mulberry paper 3¾ in x 5½ in
- Cream card 3½ in x 5 in
- Clear embossing ink pad
- Gold embossing powder

STAMPS *Oval floral frame*

- Watercolors
- Deckle-edged scissors
- Glue
- Heat tool

1 Using the embossing ink print the floral frame stamp onto the tracing paper and emboss with the gold powder.

2 Place the embossed tracing paper face down on a piece of light colored paper and color in the back of the design with watercolors.

3 Fold the white card and reopen. Position the mulberry paper on the front of the white card and glue in place.

4 Trim the cream card using the deckle-edged scissors, position over the mulberry paper and secure in place.

5 To finish, trim the tracing paper using the deckle-edged scissors, position on the cream card and secure in place.

T-SHIRT PRINTING

A dd your own touch of color and design to any plain T-shirt. To make this rosy 'T' the following will be required:

- White cotton T-shirt (washed and pressed)
- Pink fabric ink
- Green fabric ink

STAMPS *Large rose, Small rose, Small leaf*

❶ Before printing, plan out the design to ensure the pattern will fit.

❷ Protect the front of the shirt from the back with a piece of card, and begin printing. Starting with the large rose, print a single pink rose in the center of the neckline.

❸ Using the smaller rose print two pink roses, evenly spaced on either side of the large rose. Ink the leaf stamp with the green fabric ink and fill in between the roses.

❹ Once the neckline is finished, turn over the shirt and print a small leaf in green and a pink rose by the hem as a finishing touch.

SALT BOX

T o decorate this Shaker-style salt box the following
will be required:

- Salt box (unfinished)
- Sandpaper
- Embossing ink pad (or black pigment ink)
- Black embossing powder (use clear powder if using black ink
- Felt-tip pens: red, green and blue

STAMPS *Tulip border, Tiny butterfly, Mouse with tulip*

- Paint brush
- Heat tool

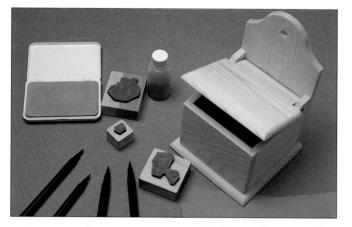

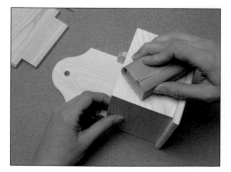

❶ If possible remove the lid and sand the surfaces of the box until smooth.

❷ Plan the pattern, then ink the tulip stamp and print onto the lower front face of the box. Ink and print a second time. Also ink and print a tiny butterfly on the same side of the box.

❸ Pour embossing powder over the images and use the paint brush to brush away any excess powder. Then heat. Repeat the pattern and process on the remaining two side faces.

❹ Ink and print the mouse stamp on the upper front face, powder and heat. Then print a butterfly onto the left corner of the lid, and emboss.

❺ Once the embossing is complete, reassemble the box and finish by coloring in the images with the felt-tip pens.

BATHROOM FRIEZE

To print this seascape frieze for your bathroom walls the following items will be required:

- Plain wallpaper frieze (measure to required length for room)

  STAMPS *Large scallop, Large conch, Small angel fish, Seaweed*

- Inks or paints (water based): green, royal blue, cyan, turquoise and old rose

1 Plan your pattern first, then begin printing. Using green ink, print the seaweed. Next, using turquoise ink, print the angel fish at the top of the frieze. Print the next fish in old rose, to the right of the first fish and in the center of the frieze. Using the cyan, print a third fish to the right of the second one and near the bottom of the frieze. Repeat the seaweed in green.

2 Ink the large scallop in navy blue, and position in the center of the frieze and print. Print a green seaweed and repeat the fish pattern. Print another green seaweed and follow that with a print of the large conch shell in navy blue. Repeat the sequence until the required length has been printed.

BIRTHDAY CAKE

Add a festive feel by creating your own birthday decorations on a plain cake. To create this jolly cake the following will be required:

- A cake iced with fondant icing. This project will work best on firm cakes, because of the necessary pressure on the cake from the stamping.
- Food coloring felt-tip pens, assorted bright colors

STAMPS *Carefree clown, Round balloon, Long balloon*

1 Using the felt-tip pens ink the balloon stamps and print in a random pattern around the side of the cake. To print, color the rubber trying to keep the color moist. Press lightly into the icing. Try to vary the colors for interest.

2 Color the clown stamp with the brightest colored pens and, again, keep the colors on the stamp moist before printing onto the top of the cake.

EARRINGS

*T*hese unusual lizard earrings would make a unique gift. To make these earrings the following will be required:

- Black fabric ink (or permanent ink)
- Sheet of shrink plastic
- Sandpaper
- Colored pencils: red, blue and green
- Gold pigment ink
- Gold embossing powder

STAMPS *Lizard*

- Scissors
- Hole punch
- Earring findings
- Pliers
- Heat tool
- Oven

❶ Score the shrink plastic lightly with sandpaper. Using the fabric ink, print two lizards onto the sanded side of the plastic.

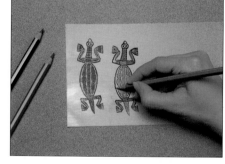

❷ Color in the images, using the colored pencils.

❸ Carefully cut out each lizard, then punch a hole in the center of the head. Place the lizards onto a baking tray and place in a pre-heated 225°F oven for 3–5 minutes. When shrunk, remove and flatten if necessary.

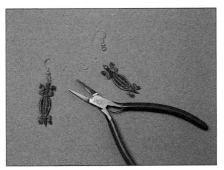

4 Ink the back of each lizard, using the gold pigment ink. Place onto a piece of paper inked side up and pour the gold embossing powder over the lizards. Heat the embossing powder until melted.

5 Finish the earrings by attaching the findings using the hole punched earlier.

NECKLACE

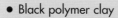

This exotic creation would add interest to any wardrobe. To make this necklace the following will be required:

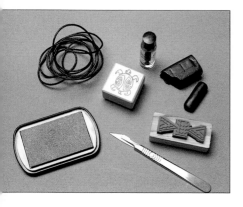

- Black polymer clay
- Gold pigment ink

STAMPS *Turtle, Aztec border*

- Black leather cord: 24 in long
- Varnish
- Craft knife
- Smooth ceramic tile

1 Knead a small piece of clay until it is soft. Roll into a ball and press it out flat onto the tile.

2 Ink the turtle stamp in gold and print onto the flattened clay.

3 Using the craft knife, carefully cut out the turtle.

4 Make a small log with the offcuts. Bend and secure underneath the turtle leaving a small hole so that the leather cord can be threaded through later.

5 To make the beads, take another piece of clay, knead and roll it into a log 1½ in long and ½ in diameter. Carefully cut it into four equal pieces.

6 Ink the center section of the border stamp with the gold ink and print onto both sides of the log pieces. Repeat the printing on the other side of each piece. Using a cocktail stick carefully make a hole through the center of each bead. Place the turtle and the beads onto a baking tray and follow the manufacturer's instructions for baking.

7 Once cooled, coat with varnish and allow to dry. To assemble, thread the turtle onto the leather cord, position in the center and knot the leather on either side. Tie another two knots approximately 1 in on either side of the turtle. Thread a bead onto each side and secure with another knot. Repeat the knotting and threading with the remaining two beads and finish by knotting the two ends together.

PAPERS

The type of paper chosen can make a difference to the final results of a project. The variety of papers available is very diverse and this is just a selection of some of the different types available.

TISSUE PAPER *Tissue is ideal for making wrapping paper and comes in a wide range of colors. It is also a very porous paper and endorsing inks will bleed through. The translucency of the paper makes it ideal for using as a decorative background paper.*

MULBERRY PAPER *This paper is like tissue paper, with a fibrous texture. Mulberry can be used to print and emboss on and it is also ideal as a decorative background paper. A nice feathering to the edge can be achieved when the paper is torn.*

TRACING PAPER *Usually used for design and drafting, this translucent paper is ideal for creating a Victorian look. Designs can be embossed onto the paper and color can be applied to the front or to the back of the paper. Vibrant colors applied to the back of the paper create a rich frosted effect to the finished design.*

RECYCLED PAPERS *There is a large variety of recycled papers on the market and each has its own properties. Some recycled papers are very absorbent and may not be suitable for printing or embossing. The Italian papers used in the combining designs project have both a smooth side and a rough side. The smooth side is ideal for printing and embossing, whereas printing onto the rough side will bleed. When selecting a recycled paper it is advisable to experiment with a piece of the paper before beginning a project to judge what the results may be.*

COLORED PAPERS *There are many different types
of colored papers and an art supply shop will usually have a
large selection to choose from. Again, a smooth finish to the
paper will give the best results. These papers are usually
available in different weights. As textures affect the finished
design, colors too, will also play an important part. If possible
test different ink colors on the paper to decide how to achieve
the best results.*

HANDMADE PAPERS *Like recycled papers, the
results will vary depending on the paper. Embossing onto
handmade papers may not give good results but again it is
best to test a small area before starting a project.*

ACKNOWLEDGMENTS

The Publishers are grateful to the following suppliers and copyright holders for permission to use their stamps in this book:

M. Findlater
BLUE CAT TOY
Builders Yard
Silver Street
South Cerney
Gloucestershire GL7 5TS
Tel: (44-185) 861867
Stamps used in Shrink plastic jewelry project: RS492F African Lizard

Diane Butler
FIRST CLASS STAMPS
Hall Staithe
Fakenham
Norfolk NR21 9BW
Tel: (44-328) 851449
Stamps used in T-shirt project: "Decorstamp" 033c small rose, 034c small rose leaf, 027f large rose Stamps used in 3D technique: 014h single rose

George Cook
FUNSTAMPS LTD
144 Neilston Road
Paisley
Scotland PA2 6QJ
Tel: (44-141) 884 6441
Stamps used in cake decoration project: FR03 carefree clown

Jennifer Mayes
HOBBY ART
St Nicholas Centre
Level 2
St Nicholas Way
Sutton
Surrey SM1 1AY
Tel: (44-181) 642 1003
Stamps used in party bag project: MS3E This book belongs to (frame stamp)

Max Osmond
INCA STAMP
136 Stanley Road
Poole
Dorset BH15 3AH
Tel: (44-1202) 669445
Stamps used in Printing on walls techniques: 626e seaweed stencil Bathroom frieze project: 474d small fish stencil, 624j large shell stencil, 6271 large shell stencil, 626e seaweed stencil Wrapping paper project: 861b floral paisley

Julie Bixley
T.N. LAWRENCE & SONS LTD
117–119 Clerkenwell Road
London EC1R 5BY
Suppliers of paper

Ainslie Claire Waller
MAKE YOUR MARK
72 Goodramgate
York YO1 2LF
Tel: (44-1904) 637355
Stamps used in Stationery project: A3687i, A3690i and A235h Stamps used in Watercolor picture project: L284711, L2858g, L2857g, L2863f, L2859f, L2875j, L28783f, L2877e, L2862h, L2865f, L2863f, L2824i, L2846i

RUBBER STAMPEDE (UK)
Unit 8
Ashburton Trading Estate
Ross on Wye
Herefordshire HR9 7BW
Tel: (44-1989) 768988
Stamps used in Reverse image technique: Mirror image stamp Embossing technique: A257H Quilt star Stained glass technique: A256H Quilt basket

Mike Payne
STAMPS UNLIMITED
16 The Frances
Thatcham
Berks RG13 3LT
Tel: (44-1635) 868990
Stamps used in Watercolor picture project: S113x Stile Wedding invitation project: BB26zz Oval floral frame

Jennie Hulme
THE STAMP CONNECTION
14 Edith Road
Faversham
Kent ME13 8SD
Tel: (44-1795) 531860
Stamps used in Printing on wood technique: E483 Apple, E484 Cherries Gift Tag project: B520 Maple leaf Combining designs project: D475 Fan seaweed, D476 seaweed Bookmark project: H369 Sunflower Necklace project: D664 Aztec turtle, E667 Aztec border

All other stamps used in the book were designed by
Terri Earl-McEwen
149 East Queen Street
Pendleton
South Carolina 29670
USA
Tel: (803) 646 9431

These designs are available worldwide; contact Terri for your nearest distributor.